T0150241

SPIN FISHING
BASICS

SPIN FISHING
BASICS

Francis P. Pandolfi
and Jono Pandolfi

Burford Books

Printed in the United States of America.

10 9 8 7 6 5 4 3 2 1

Library of Congress Cataloging-in-Publication Data
    Pandolfi, Francis P., 1943–
    Spin fishing basics / Francis P. Pandolfi and Jono Pandolfi.
        p.   cm.
    ISBN 978-1-58080-150-8
    1. Spin fishing. I. Pandolfi, Jono, 1976– II. Title.

SH456.5.P36   2008
799.12'6—dc22

                            2007052473

To Joyce, who never asks us to pull the weeds,
vacuum the rugs, fill the dishwasher,
or do *anything* before fishing.

CONTENTS

CONTENTS

CONTENTS

CONTENTS

SPIN FISHING
BASICS

1

WHAT IS SPIN FISHING?

Using a spinning rod and reel is a lot of fun, and you need only a few easy instructions before you're ready to enjoy it.

The lures you cast might be diving lures that you reel in below the surface of the water, or they may be floating lures retrieved across its surface. Which way to go depends on what the fish are up to. Once you know how to use spinning gear, you can use it just as often for bait fishing—casting out your bait, perhaps with a bobber, and letting it sit there until a fish finds it.

There are two kinds of spinning reels. The first is the kind shown on the cover of this book, and that's what we'll talk about here. The other—called a spin-cast reel— has a cover over the line controlled by a button. You hold down this button until you swing the rod during your cast; then you release it, and the line flows out from under the cover. The spin-cast reel is really more for young beginners. There are also bait-casting reels. These are a different animal altogether: A moving line guide assures a smooth cast or retrieve by guiding the line back and forth across the spool. These reels tend to be harder to get used to than the spinning reels we'll discuss here.

2

PURCHASING EQUIPMENT FOR THE FIRST TIME

To choose the proper spinning gear, you need to decide what kinds of fish you'll be going after. For example, large saltwater fish will require gear somewhat heavier than what you'll use for freshwater fish, which are typically a bit smaller. When you get started, of course, you don't want to have to buy several rods and reels for different types of fishing, so choose gear that will be a good all-purpose combination. Whether you plan to use bait or lures doesn't matter in this decision.

The three most important things you need to buy are a rod, a reel, and line, all described below. Chapter 7 will give you the details on some of the other gear you'll need to get started.

ROD

Probably the best rod to start with is one designed for 10- to 15-pound-test line. (Line is described by its breaking strength. A 10-pound-test line, for example, will break only if more than 10 pounds of pull is applied to it.) Ideally, it will be 6 or 7 feet long and come in two or three pieces; such rods are a lot easier to carry around than one-piece models. Virtually all good rods have this information printed right next to the handle. Most rods today are made out of graphite, which is durable and flexible.

If you intend to use your rod mainly in salt water, it's worth buying a slightly more expensive model with better materials, since salt water corrodes just about everything in sight. In general, a good starter rod can be purchased for about $50 to $80.

REEL

Choosing a good reel is as important as choosing a good rod. The most important feature of a good spinning reel is its "drag." The drag on a spinning reel is adjustable; when you have a fish on, you can vary the tension—as the line is pulled from the reel—from light to heavy. The fish, that is, will draw line off the reel spool if the drag is set light enough; it will be unable to pull out line with a heavy drag setting. What's the point? Well, you may need to adjust the reel's tension so that the fish *pulls* off line instead of *breaking* it off.

The critical factor in a drag is that it be smooth, not jerky. When the fish is pulling line, it should flow smoothly off the spool rather than jerking off in short and uneven strips. Unfortunately, it's very difficult to tell if a reel has a smooth drag when you're purchasing it, because it may be wrapped in a plastic packaging (you know the kind—you need a hacksaw to cut it open). The best thing you can do is to ask the store clerk. But decent reels likely to have a suitable drag can be purchased for $50 to $75. Some very high-quality spinning reels cost more than $500—but those are for a later stage in life! Also note that there are very good rod-and-reel combos for sale at many stores and in catalogs starting at about $100 (lower-priced combos are unlikely to be satisfactory with a lot of usage).

The size of your reel depends on what you intend to fish for and on how much line you can put on the spool. That, in turn, is a function of the line's pound test; stronger lines are thicker, and thus less will fit on a reel. Large fish may pull off quite a bit of line, whereas small ones won't. On the other hand, it's seldom useful to buy a reel that can store 300 yards of line: Any fish that can pull off that much against a tight drag is almost certainly going to keep going until it breaks the line right off the spool. So a good all-around line might have a 12-pound breaking strength, and the reel will be filled with about 250 yards. Line capacities for different test strengths are marked on all good reels. The advantage of a light line is that you can cast a small, light lure a long distance. Longer casts cover more water and can often get you better results.

LINE

When you purchase line, buy enough to fill the reel that you bought. Two hundred fifty yards should be more than enough. Spools are clearly marked with the line's breaking strength and length. While there are several types of spinning line, you might start with monofilament (a type of plastic); this is easy to put on your reel and easy to tie knots with. Other types of braided lines are becoming more popular these days, but they aren't as easy to use as monofilament—and monofilament is usually a lot less expensive. One of the characteristics of monofilament line (or "mono") is that it stretches; braided line does not. To some extent, then, you can set a hook more firmly when a fish strikes with braid than with mono. But for newer fishermen, this isn't an important advantage.

To start out, you're looking for a 12-pound-breaking-strength line (designed to break if the pull is stronger than 12 pounds), or possibly 15 pounds at most. The lighter line will allow you to make longer casts with lighter lures and is unlikely to break unless you've tied a bad knot or your drag is too tight. A good line that you can trust will cost about $6 to $7.

Here's one other little trick you can use in the early going: If for some reason you lose a large batch of line, you don't necessarily have to get rid of *all* the line on the spool to refill it to the proper level—more on that later. You can tie new line to what's left on the spool using the blood knot described in the next section. But if you do this, be sure to use eight or nine wraps of the line rather than just five (this is explained on page 16).

3
LET'S GO FISHING!

KNOTS

There are really only three or four knots you must know to get started. There are plenty of books you can buy with these and many other knots well illustrated, but we'll show you enough to begin right here.

ARBOR KNOT. Use this easy knot to tie your line to the reel.

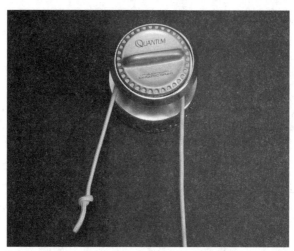

Tie an overhand knot in the end of your line, pull the knot tight, and slip the line around the reel spool.

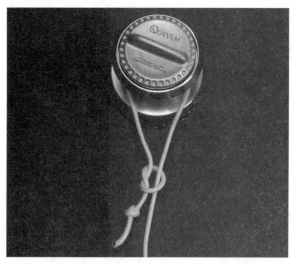

Now tie a second overhand knot over the line that feeds back to the spool of line you purchased (this is called the "standing" line). Pull that knot tight also. Trim the extra line coming off the first overhand knot (this is called the "tag" end of the line), then pull on the standing line until the two knots come together and slide up against the reel spool.

IMPROVED CLINCH KNOT. Use this strong knot to tie swivels or lures directly to your line.

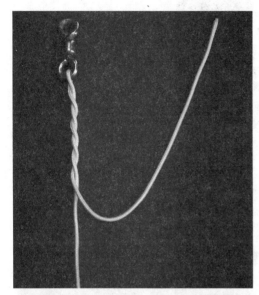

Run the line through the swivel, hook eye (if you're bait fishing), or lure eye that you want to tie onto your line, and wrap the tag end around the standing line about six times.

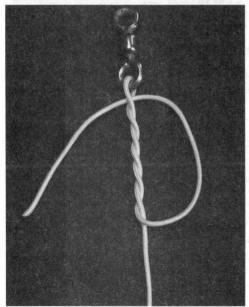

Now run the tag end through the opening in the line closest to the swivel, hook eye, or lure eye to create a large loop.

Feed the tag end through the large loop.

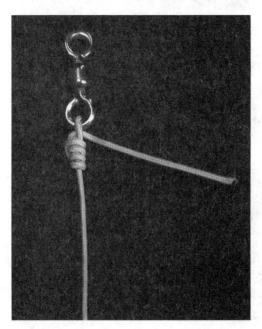

Pull alternately on the standing line and the tag end until the knot comes tight—but before you do that, moisten the line with some saliva, which will allow the line to slide smoothly to a tight knot. Finally, cut off the tag end. You're ready to go.

LOOP KNOT. This is another easy knot that you can use to tie your lure directly to the line. Use this knot if you have a heavy monofilament on your reel (perhaps 20-pound breaking strength or greater)—it will keep the line from damping the lure's action. Some lures need to move freely in the water to have the desired effect, and this knot allows them to do so.

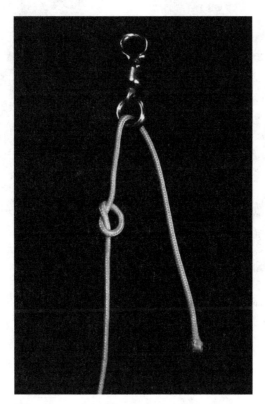

Tie an overhand knot in the line—but don't pull it tight yet—and feed the tag end through the lure eye.

13

Now feed the tag end through the original overhand knot.

Using the tag end that you just pulled through the first knot, tie a second overhand knot, this one over the standing part of the line.

14

Finally, pull each knot tight, then pull on the standing part of the line until the two knots come together. Cut off the tag end right at the knot.

BLOOD KNOT. This knot isn't easy at first, but it is the best way for you to tie one piece of monofilament line to another, perhaps if the line were to break. It's also a pretty good knot for tying heavier line to lighter line as long as the difference in thicknesses isn't too great.

15

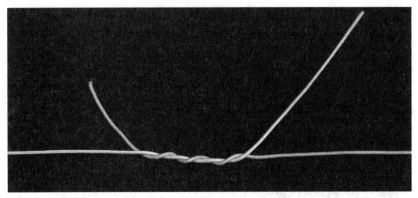

Start by twisting the two lines around each other about 5 times (or more—up to 10 times—if you are comfortable doing so). Leave one tag end longer than the other.

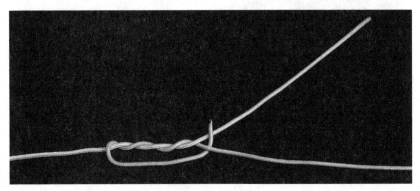

Take the shorter tag end, bring it to the other end of the twisted line, and place it as shown.

Next, take the longer tag end and twist it around the standing line as many times as you twisted the lines together to start with.

Now bring this longer tag end back to the center of the knot and feed it through the opening in the center of the twisted lines so that it enters in the direction opposite the way you fed through the first tag end.

Finally, pull on both standing lines, and the knot will tighten up. But be sure to moisten the line with saliva before you pull. This procedure takes some patience and dexterity: The two tag ends will try their best to slip out of the center opening as you're drawing the knot tight.

PUTTING THE REEL ONTO THE ROD

Spinning reels are mounted *below* the rod. Here's how:

WHICH HAND SHOULD I REEL WITH? This tends to be a matter of personal preference. You can remove the handle on most good reels and remount it on the side you prefer. Typically, you do this by taking off a screw that holds the handle to the reel, flipping the handle over to the other side of the reel, and reattaching the screw. Consider starting by reeling with the hand most comfortable for you; you can always change the position of the handle later. Most right-handed people actually turn the reel handle with their left hand.

Loosen the handle screw and remove it completely before pulling out the reel handle and placing it in on the opposite side of the reel. Then reinsert the handle screw opposite to where it was originally and tighten.

MOUNTING THE REEL ON THE ROD. Spinning reels can be mounted to the rod in various ways. Whatever you do, be sure to tighten the mounting ring; otherwise, your reel may end up in the water!

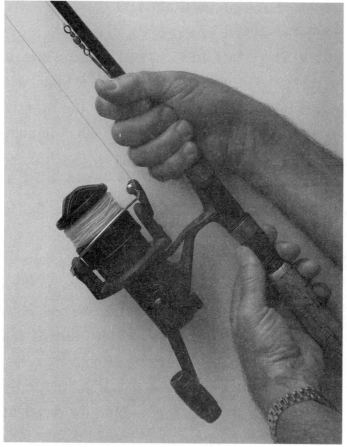

Tighten the mounting ring so the reel is firmly in place.

PUTTING LINE ONTO THE REEL

This is a little more interesting than you might think at first. The steps are these:

FEED THE LINE ON THE ROD. Take the line and run it down through the guides to the reel.

TIE THE LINE TO THE REEL SPOOL. Be sure that the bail on the reel is *open,* and tie the line to the spool with the arbor knot described earlier. The bail is the wire that circles halfway around the spool of line. It will be flipped open when you cast, closed when you reel in.

LOAD THE LINE ONTO THE SPOOL. Close the bail by starting to crank the reel handle, and you're ready to spool the line onto the reel. *The line must come off the plastic spool you purchased and onto the reel by unwinding off the plastic spool in exactly the same way it winds onto the reel spool.* That is, if the line goes onto the reel clockwise, it must come off the spool clockwise. This is very important; otherwise, your line will twist as it goes onto the reel. Run the line through your fingers to be sure that it goes onto the reel tightly. As you reel in the line, the drag should be set tightly enough so that the line will come smoothly through your fingers. If your fingers are too tight, the reel spool may be turning without picking up any line. This will further twist your line.

The line must come off the spool unwinding in the same direction that it winds onto the reel spool.

Keep tension on the line as you reel it onto the spool.

One other way to get the line onto the reel is to let the clerk do it in the store where you buy your rod and reel. It's a service most good tackle shops provide at no cost when you buy line.

HOW MUCH LINE TO LOAD. Most spools that you purchase will have more than enough line to fill your reel spool. Fill the reel spool to within about ⅛ inch of the lip of the reel spool.

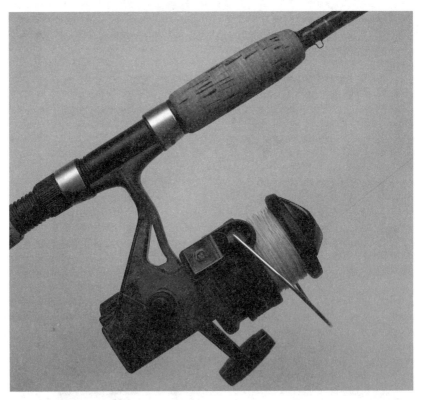

This is a properly loaded reel spool.

KEEPING THE LINE ON THE REEL. Once you've loaded the line, there are two ways to keep it on the reel if you're not going to fish right away. You can either tie on a swivel and then attach the snap to the hook keeper located next to the handle; or, if your rod doesn't have a hook keeper, attach the swivel to one of the rod's line guides. Alternatively, you can reel the line all the way in through the rod guides and put an elastic band over the reel spool to keep it from unwinding. Many reels also have a plastic tab on the side of the spool to which you can attach the line.

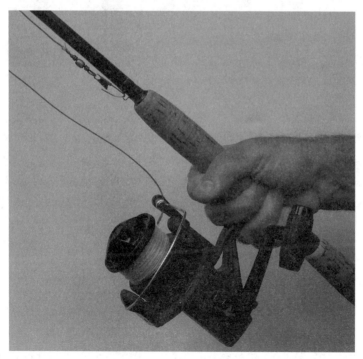

The swivel is attached to the hook keeper to keep the line from unwinding and tangling.

In this case, use a thick rubber band to keep the line from unwinding off the spool.

CHECKING YOUR LINE. Periodically, you should perform three checks on your line:

- Every now and then, run the last 10 yards of line through your fingers to see if you feel any nicks. If you can feel and possibly see a nick, cut the line at that point and tie on your swivel again. The line can get nicked or abraded in many ways; it always pays to check on it so that it doesn't break at the wrong moment. When disposing of old line, be sure to put it in a waste container. Do not drop it into the water.

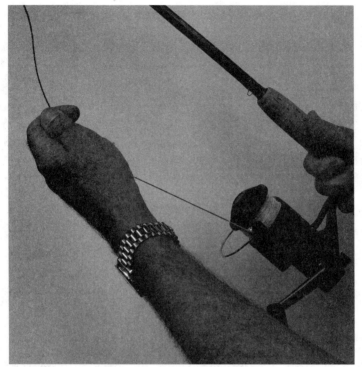

Running the line through your fingers will allow you to feel if there are any nicks that might weaken it.

- Second, check to see if your line has become twisted. If it has, this can ruin your casts or retrieves. The way to check for twist is to cast the line out and then, before reeling it in, form a large loop near the reel and see if it twists upon itself. If it does and you have a boat, remove the lure and drag a long length of line behind the vessel while moving slowly; the line will untwist itself. Unfortunately, there are no really good ways to remove twist without a boat.

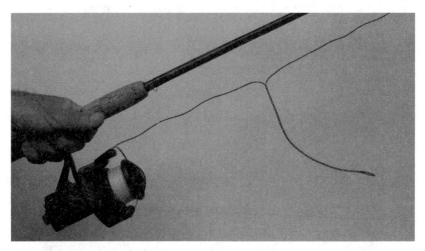

If your line is twisted, it will wrap over itself.

• Finally, note the moment when—after you've periodically cut off pieces of line, or broken the line when you're
hung up on a rock, say—it only fills about two-thirds of
the reel spool. At this point, it's time to replace the line
with a new full spool (or to tie on additional line using the
blood knot). This allows you to cast longer distances.

This spool needs more line.

TYING ON A LURE

Use an improved clinch knot or loop knot to tie your swivel or lure to the line. It's wise to moisten the knot with some saliva before pulling it tight so that it will slide smoothly into place. Always cut off the tag end after you pull down the knot. A properly tied knot will not slip, and if you leave much of a piece of line hanging off the knot, it will invariably pick up weed as it comes through the water—something most fish find unattractive!

SETTING THE DRAG ON THE REEL

To get started, adjust the drag so that you can pull line from the reel relatively easily. It should take a bit of a pull to get the line out—but not too much of a pull. Typically, you don't need to change the drag when you catch a fish, though you might loosen it a bit when the fish gets near the boat. Monofilament line has quite a bit of stretch, which makes it difficult for the fish to break it if the drag is properly set; still, there's less stretch when the fish gets near the boat, and you'll want a looser drag to help you keep the line from breaking.

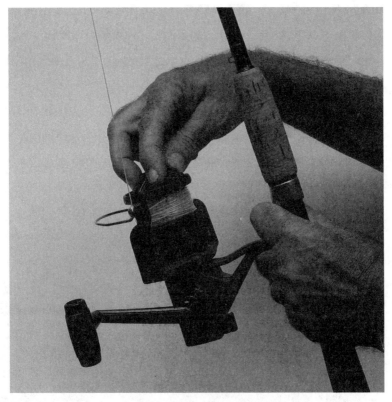

The drag knob is most often located at the spool, but on some reels it may be at the back.

PREPARING TO CAST

Mastering casting is the secret to having fun with spin fishing. Here's what you need to know:

CHECK THE HOOKS. Periodically check the points of your hooks to make sure they're sharp and that they haven't been bent if the lure got hung up on a rock.

LOCKING ONE-WAY TURNING. Spinning-reel handles can turn in both directions; you want to be sure that you have moved the small lever on the reel that locks the handle-turning direction so that it can only reel line *in*. Otherwise, you may start to reel in the wrong direction and find that the line is going out when it should be coming in!

Find the switch that controls the turning of the reel handle and put it in the position that allows the handle to turn in only one direction.

PULL SOME LINE OUT. Pull out a bit of line so that the lure is hanging from the end of the rod along with a foot or more of line. Enough should be hanging from the rod tip so that no knots or swivels have gone through the guides. (If they have, the friction of the knot or swivel passing through the guides will shorten your cast. This isn't a big deal for knots, but it *is* for swivels, which can scratch or damage your guides if they pass through with the force from a strong cast.) You can easily pull out the line by grabbing it just in front of the reel and pulling. It will be coming off against the pressure of the drag so it will feel a bit tight, but that's fine.

About a foot of line hangs from the rod tip prior to casting.

THE GRIP. Hold the rod over the reel mount in the hand that you're most comfortable casting with. Position the post that mounts the reel on the rod between your fingers for a stronger grip.

For the best grip, the leg that holds the reel to the rod should be between your fingers.

The next three things you have to do are probably where most beginners have the most trouble. Remember them with the letters: **RFO.**

ROTATE THE SPOOL. Rotate the spool with your hand (turning against the drag) so that the line is coming off the top of the spool, between the spool and the rod.

The line must come off the spool nearest to the rod.

PUT THE LINE OVER YOUR FINGER. Put the line over the *tip* of your index finger so that the line comes directly off the top of the spool toward the rod. You don't have to press the line against the rod handle with your finger, although you can if you want to. Later you'll find that you have more control over the cast if you don't pin the line against the rod handle.

33

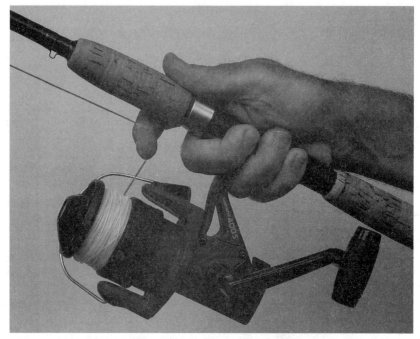

Pull the line toward the rod with your index finger. Now you can open the bail as shown here.

OPEN THE BAIL. Flip the bail to the open position. If you're holding the line with your finger correctly, it won't come off the spool.

With the bail open, the line will flow off the reel spool when you cast.

You'll discover that if you skip the **R** step and you open the bail before the line is positioned to come off the top of the spool, a few—or even many—turns of line will come off. You'll have to rewind those before you can start again with the line coming off the top.

THE CAST ITSELF

You can cast with one hand or two, depending on how far you want to throw the lure. But when you are first learning, it's wise to practice with short casts; you can move on to longer ones later when you've started to perfect your technique.

- Short casts—use only wrist action.
- Medium casts—use wrist and arm action.
- Long casts—use both hands and arms.

THE STARTING POSITION. Although you can position the rod off to your side when you're getting ready to cast (and you may have to do this if there are any obstructions behind you), you should start by putting it directly back over your shoulder.

Holding the rod with one hand, position it over your shoulder.

You can also hold the rod with both hands and position it over your shoulder.

It's sometimes desirable to cast sidearm if there's an obstacle behind you.

THE SWING. Make it smooth and not too fast as you get started.

Swing the rod in the direction you want to cast.

THE RELEASE POINT. This is where you release your finger and allow the line to shoot out over the water. By the way, if you're using live bait, don't cast as if you want to set a world record—the bait might tear right off the hook.

Release your finger when the rod is in this position.

DIRECTION OF THE CAST. You will want the ability to cast your lure or bait in a particular direction where you think there are fish. To improve your direction, start by making short casts at first—maybe only 25 feet. The lure will go in the direction you want if you swing the rod that way with its tip moving from behind you to in front of you.

REELING IN THE LURE

HOW FAST TO RETRIEVE. A lure coming through the water should look realistic—and a super-fast retrieve seldom achieves this effect. Take a look at the lure's movement through the water when it's near you, then see what it looks like when you adjust your speed. Most lures will waggle back and forth, and this action should be slow and smooth. Some lures do require a fast retrieve; this may be indicated on the packaging when you buy the lure, or you can ask the owner of the tackle shop. If you're bait fishing, you'll probably want to attach a bobber or float to the line and then just leave it motionless in the water until a fish finds it. The float should generally be positioned far enough up the line to keep the bait dangling in open water (not sitting on the bottom). If the float is too far up the line and the bait lies on the bottom, the float will probably turn on its side; whenever you see this, reel in and reset the bobber closer to the hook.

STARTING TO REEL IN. Start to turn the handle (thus automatically closing the bail) just *before* the lure hits the water. This will prevent line from coming off the spool after the lure hits the water and possibly forming a loop at the spool when you start your retrieve. Note that the minute you start to turn the handle, the bail automatically flips over to guide the line onto the spool—and also remember that sometimes the handle may be hard to start turning, but once it does start, it'll be very smooth. One other tip: Don't reel the lure or hook all the way back to the top guide (called the "tip-top" guide). Always leave some line hanging free.

POINTING THE ROD. Hold the rod either pointing at the line you are reeling in or in a slightly elevated position. Do not point the rod off to the side when you're reeling in.

This is the proper way to hold the rod when you're reeling in.

BAIT FISHING

Fishing with bait is every bit as popular as fishing with lures. Live bait can be purchased at many tackle stores, and that's also the place to go for tips on what works best. But live bait also has the advantage of being available in your backyard, a local brook, or by the beach and docks, depending on what you're fishing for. Collecting live bait provides an adventure in addition to the adventure of fishing itself!

FRESH WATER. Probably the most popular bait for freshwater anglers is the old standby—the worm. And worms come in lots of sizes, starting with the garden variety that you can find in the dirt almost everywhere. At the large end of the scale is the nightcrawler; this fellow can be 6 or 7 inches long. Did you ever wonder why they are called nightcrawlers? Well, it's because they're easy to find on a lawn—especially a golf course lawn—at night, particularly after a rain. If you have your own lawn, water it well in the afternoon and then go out at night to get your bait. All you need to do this is a flashlight and a can with some loose soil and grass in it to hold your catch. But if you're collecting your own nightcrawlers, you'd better be fast: They will head back into the dirt when they see the light approaching or if they feel the vibrations from your heavy footsteps. This takes some practice!

Be sure to keep your worms or nightcrawlers in a cool, dark spot with loose soil. Use a larger can to prevent the worms from becoming too compact. When you put them on your hook, just put the hook through them in three or four places, leaving a lively end to dangle off where it can wiggle to attract fish. After all, since fish don't normally eat worms on the lawn, they must be attracted by the wiggle. Consider breaking the nightcrawlers in half—you seldom need such a large bait. Garden worms are probably best for trout, while larger worms are great for bass, perch, pickerel, catfish, sunfish, crappies, or other species.

You can also search nearby brooks for crayfish—great bait, especially for bass. These maneuverable creatures are hard to catch, although it's worthwhile if you can do it. To fish with one, put the hook through the tail; it'll move about to attract fish.

There are many kinds of minnows that are also good bait for trout, bass, and other fish, but they're best purchased at the tackle store. Hooking minnows—which go by many names, including sawbellies—is best done through the lips or the back.

Rigging your line for live bait is pretty simple. Typically, you'll put a lead sinker on the line about a foot above the hook, then attach a bobber a few feet above that so that the bait is suspended in the water; there, its movement will attract your quarry. But sometimes you want the bait right on the bottom—for example, with crayfish. In that case, eliminate the sinker and the bobber, hook on the crayfish, and cast it to the hot spot. One problem with this is that the crayfish often crawl under the rocks—which is where bass often hang out—and they might get your hook caught on the rock. But that's just part of fishing!

Keep in mind that trout, in particular, can be enticed by a bread ball or even a kernel of corn on the hook. All you need to do to make these baits work is keep them jiggling in the water.

SALT WATER. There's a greater variety of bait for saltwater fish. And more often in salt water than fresh, the bait might be used even after it has died. Saltwater baits range from worms (bloodworms and sandworms are the most popular); to live eels (which may be 12 to 18 inches long); to clams (what's inside, not the shell); to all sorts of baitfish. One of the most popular baits is the menhaden, also called bunker and many other names depending on where you fish. Menhaden can be bought frozen and cut up to be put on the hook one piece at a time. Another highly popular baitfish, mainly in the southeastern United States, is the mullet, also available at bait-and-tackle stores. Squid, too, is used often; it can be bought frozen and cut up.

If you're going to use live minnows, keep in mind that you'll need to keep them in a bucket of water, and the water must be aerated or changed regularly to keep your bait alive. It helps to have a small net available to catch these creatures—they have a way of escaping through your fingers.

Along rock jetties and on pilings under and around docks, you can find mussels and snails that, when extracted from their shells, make good bait. Likewise, these areas sometimes offer small crabs, which particularly interest striped bass.

There tend to be some more complex rigging systems in salt water than in fresh. You're best off going to your local tackle store for advice.

By the way, if you're going to fish with live bait, bring a rag with you. You'll need it!

CATCHING AND RELEASING THE FISH

HOOKING THE FISH. When the fish strikes, you don't need to yank the rod back with great force. A quick and moderate pull on the rod will do it.

WHEN *NOT* TO REEL IN. One of the most difficult things for beginners to remember is *not* to reel in when the fish is pulling out line against the drag. You'll always know when the fish is pulling out line: Your reel will make a clicking sound. Only reel when the fish isn't pulling line out, or you'll badly twist your line. At all times keep pressure on the fish by keeping the rod bent a bit.

PUMP AND REEL. The best way to reel in, especially if you have a sizable fish, is to pump the rod up and then reel only as you move the rod down.

Pump the rod up without reeling as you bring in your fish.

Reel as you lower the rod.

NETTING THE FISH. Raise your rod when the fish is near, and dip the net in the water below the fish. If you don't have a net, you can cradle the fish in your hand—just take care not to get poked by any sharp fins. *Always* wet your hand before you touch the fish, or you'll remove some of the coating from the fish's scales and create the possibility for an infection to set in. You can also take a fish out of the water by putting your thumb over its lower lip and your forefinger under the lip. But note that this is unwise if the fish has sharp teeth. (Pike and bluefish, for instance, cannot be handled this way.)

RELEASING THE FISH. If you don't plan to keep your catch, be sure to handle it gently as you remove the hook and then place the fish carefully back in the water. Do not throw it back. Be gentle! Release the fish into the water and, if it has been a long fight, move it back and forth before releasing your grip. This allows water to wash over its gills, helping the fish regain its strength.

BARBLESS HOOKS

As you get more confident with your technique, consider using barbless hooks when you fish. You create barbless hooks by bending down the barbs with a pliers—and this is an especially good idea if you are using treble hooks (three hooks on a single shaft, very common with lures).

Why do this? For two very good reasons, the first of which is safety. Should you get a barbless hook in your skin, it's easy to slip it out. But if it has a barb and penetrates beyond the barb, your next stop will be the emergency room! Note, however, that if you remove a barbless hook yourself, it is always a good idea to apply some antiseptic ointment.

The other reason to fish with barbless hooks is because it's a great deal easier to get barbless hooks out of a fish you want to release. Getting the hooks out quickly and easily will likely result in a fish that will quickly recover from its ordeal.

But there's one important tip to remember with barb-less hooks: You always have to keep the pressure on the fish while reeling it in. If you don't, the hook is pretty likely to slip out, and you'll lose your catch. When fish are being reeled in, they twist, turn, and pull; all this motion makes the hole where the hook penetrated the fish's mouth get larger. Without a barb, then, the hook may well slip out of the larger hole.

4

TAKING CARE
OF YOUR GEAR

Taking good care of your gear means that it will enjoy a long life—and it's easy to do. If you're fishing mainly in salt water, you need to take particular care to clean your gear, because the salty environment is so tough on tackle.

Every so often during the fishing season, spray some WD-40 on the exterior moving parts of your reel—but don't let it get onto the line or the lures. WD-40 is a light oil lubricant available in hardware stores.

After each use, attach your lure to one of the rod guides—but don't put the hook into one of the eyes. (Pull out enough line—as described above—to reach the guide.) It can chip or scratch the eye, and that, in turn, may abrade your line. Instead, put the hook through one of the legs that holds the guide to the rod; you can also use the hook keeper that some manufacturers build onto the rod right next to the handle.

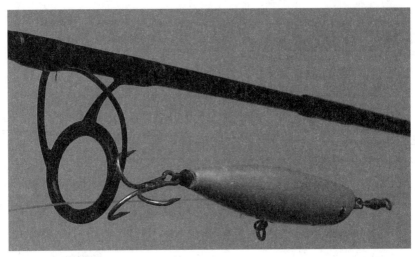

Note that the hook is not attached within the guide. It's placed on the leg that supports the guide.

Then spray down your rod, reel, and lures with fresh water using a light spray. Finally, loosen the drag, and store the gear in spot where it won't get dusty.

At the end of each season, open the side plates of the reel, remove any dirty grease, and pack the gears with Vaseline.

Always use a light spray of fresh water on your reel after use.

5
LURES

There are so many lures that we could describe here, reading about them would delay your fishing! The best way to decide what lures to purchase at first is to ask a fishing buddy what works in your area; or to talk to the clerk in your tackle store. Lures vary by length, weight, color, material (such as soft or hard plastic), and hook size. Some even have rattles inside to make noise as the lure moves through the water.

Here's a brief description of some of the most popular kinds.

PLUGS

Plugs are usually made of plastic or sometimes wood. They come in three main types: divers, swimmers, and poppers.

DIVERS usually have a lip in the front that causes them to dive deep down into the water when they're reeled in. (Obviously, these are not for use in shallow spots!)

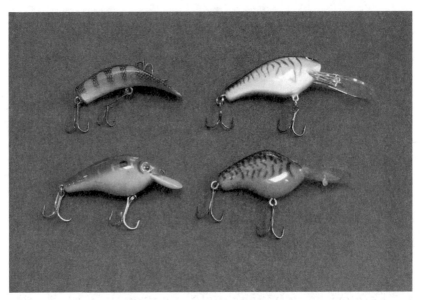

Freshwater diving lures.

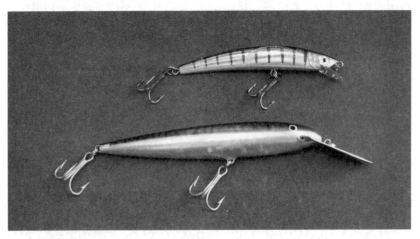

Saltwater diving lures.

SWIMMERS. These "swim" just below or at the surface of the water, usually with a waggling motion.

Commonly used swimmers.

Freshwater swimming lures.

POPPERS are retrieved with a jerking motion and create quite a commotion on the surface of the water.

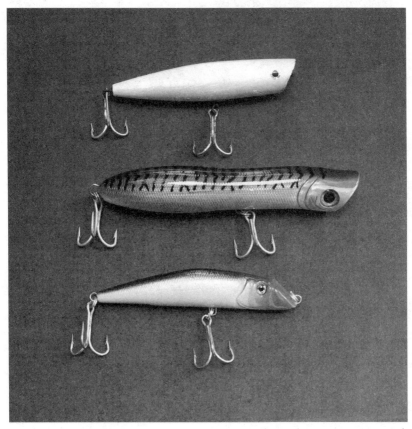

Saltwater poppers.

Freshwater poppers.

SPOONS

Spoons are metal lures that travel under the surface and usually wobble back and forth to look like a minnow.

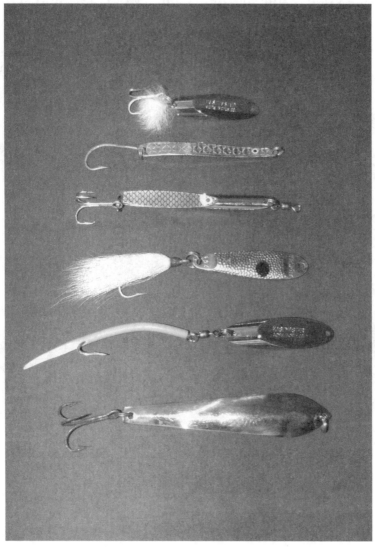

Spoons are made of metal and can be quite heavy for long casts.

SOFT BAITS

Usually plastic worms that you can attach to a hook (possibly with a lead head) or imitations of small bait fish, soft baits come in an enormous variety of colors and shapes.

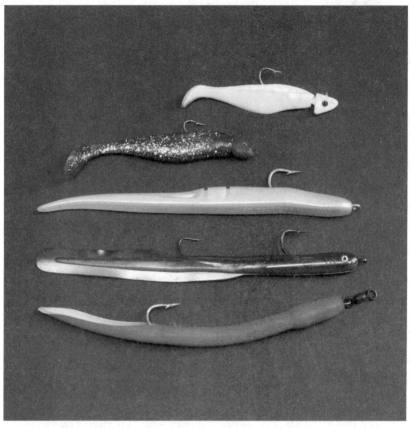

Soft plastic baits mainly used in salt water.

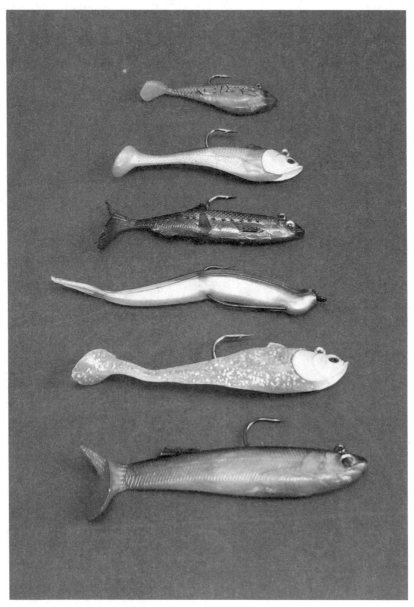

Smaller saltwater swimming lures.

JIGS

Also called bucktail jigs—after the hair attached to the lead head—these lures come in many colors and sizes and can be very effective for a large variety of fish.

Jigs have lead heads and can be cast quite a distance.

Lures can be pretty expensive, and you'll need at least a few to get started. You might pay anywhere from $3 for a package of several soft plastic-bodied lures to $8–12 for a single plastic swimming plug. So already you know that you'd better pay close attention to the comments on knots earlier in this book! Poorly tied knots can result in your losing some expensive tackle.

Remember that fish are attracted to your lure or a bait by one or more of the three S's:

• Sight.
• Sound.
• Smell.

You'll thus want a lure of the correct color and a rattle if possible (though it's not essential). As for smell, fish can naturally smell one another, and larger fish can smell the bait they're after. Some lure manufacturers make bottles of smelly liquid that you can put on your lure to make it more tempting. This isn't something you need to worry about when you're getting started, though. In fact, not very many fishermen use these attractors at all.

6
THE TIP LIST

The more observant you are when you're fishing, the more successful you can be. Whether you're in fresh water or salt, keep your eyes and ears—and even your nose—open to learn some great secrets. While we could probably write a chapter on every single one of these points, here are just a few thoughts to get you started.

THE FIVE B'S

BAIT. Fish are *always* looking for food. They never stop. So you need to be where whatever they might eat will be. In a freshwater stream or lake, the signs are less obvious than they are in the salt, where baits often break the surface and give away the location of bigger fish that may be chasing them. But in a fast-flowing stream, think like a fish. You might guess that you'd like to hide behind a rock or at the edge of a bank where the current won't push you around and tire you out—while at the same time you could watch for smaller fish or bugs flowing by you in the current.

If you can actually see the bait in the water and you're using a lure, try to use one about the same size and color as the bait.

Peanut bunker (menhaden) are a favorite saltwater baitfish.

Mackerel and herring attract many large saltwater gamefish.

BIRDS. On the water, mainly salt water, birds can be your best friends: They're often looking for exactly the same food as the fish you're after. You may find birds diving over bait—and right under the bait are the fish you're pursuing. This can happen close to beaches and shore rocks, or in open water if you're in a boat and can reach the birds. (By the way, it's possible that a bird may occasionally grab your lure or twist your line around its wing. If that happens, reel in the bird and wrap its head gently in a cloth or towel while you remove the lure or line.)

Gulls flock over baitfish.

This gull is getting splashed by a large bluefish!

Sometimes when you're fishing in salt water and the birds are thick and diving onto the water, you need to cast out your lure and let it sink a bit before retrieving it. That's because some of the largest fish will likely be hanging below the bigger school on the surface. They're waiting there for the small fish to chop up the bait and let it drift down to them.

BOATS. Other fishermen may know more than you, so look for boats—and you may well find fish. But keep in mind that proper etiquette is important. Don't get too close to your neighbors. Nor should you race around near other boats; you may scare away the fish.

Friendly neighbors—at a distance!

BREAKING. When fish get excited about the bait or the bugs they're chasing, they may well break the surface of the water and give away their location. But that doesn't mean they'll be easy to catch—they are quite preoccupied with all the food around them. Still, your chances here are far better than average.

Snapper bluefish breaking the surface.

BAROMETRIC PRESSURE. There's no question that fish are sensitive to barometric pressure, and there is no end to the theories about whether to fish when the barometer is rising or falling. In fact, there are so many theories that the best advice we can give you is this: Pay attention to when you get the best action in your area, and think about whether pressure is rising or falling. Your local Weather Channel will have that information for you all day long. This, by the way, is one of the last things someone new to the sport needs to worry about. But it is something that you'll grow accustomed to considering as you spend more time on the water.

Beware of weather fronts that can move in quickly.

THE THREE T'S

TEMPERATURE. Water temperature is a key factor in fishing, depending not only on the month but also on the time of day. Fish start feeding as the temperature rises and stop when it gets too high. In other words, there's an ideal feeding range for fish—and it varies from species to species. When you're getting started, the best thing to do is not to worry all that much about the exact temperature. Instead, observe when other people are fishing, and ask your local tackle dealer for advice.

Lots of people are convinced that it's best to start fishing just as the sun rises and the water starts to warm; and, in fact, that could be a great time to be by the water because it's really pretty then. But remember that fish are *always* hungry. If other conditions are okay, the fishing is likely to be good right through to sunset.

TIDE. While not a factor in freshwater fishing, tide is a key factor in the saltwater environment. The best time to fish is when the water is moving. Baitfish have less control over their movement in a strong current, which makes them easier pickings for the bigger fish. Many tackle stores (or even the Internet) have tide charts helping you see when the best time to fish might be in your local area. But be mindful of the fact that while tide charts are generally accurate, the actual conditions on the water can vary a lot from place to place—even when those places are close by—depending on the structure of the bottom and other factors.

If you have a boat, one thing to look for is a tide line that marks the front edge of the moving water when the tide is rising or falling. Fish often love to hang out here, because tide lines collect bait and other food particles.

Tide lines can extend for long distances and are great gathering places for fish.

TIMING. In all waters, fresh and salt, the time of year and the phase of the moon are important. Full and new moons create higher tides in salt water, and of course water temperature varies a great deal by time of year. Too, some fish migrate as a function of temperature. These are things you can learn about as you become more and more interested in this sport.

THE THREE S'S

SLICK. On salt water, if you have a boat and you come upon a slick, fish it. A slick is a patch of water that is very smooth compared with the water around it, which may be choppy. This condition is often caused by larger fish chopping up oily baitfish. As the oil spreads across the water, it smooths the surface. It often means that there are gamefish around.

SMELL. Smells often accompany a slick on salt water, where you might also smell a fishy scent anytime, thanks to the same phenomenon that causes the slick. Oily baitfish have an odor—and when you smell it, look around for slicks or for fish busting the surface of the water.

STRUCTURE is important in all kinds of water, fresh or salt. The word refers to natural or man-made objects below the surface of the water that might provide good living conditions for your fish. In streams, trout and other fish often hang around rocks, because the rocks stop the current and leave a good resting place in their lee. In salt water, *structure* may refer to rock jetties or underwater wrecks, where fish will often gather.

Branches in the water also provide structure for fish such as bass to get comfortable. Here the fish feel that they are safe from predators like large shorebirds. But these are also great places to cast and get hung up, losing your lure. It's better to avoid spots like this until your casting technique is solid.

THE TWO R'S

RIPS. In salt water, rips are formed around reefs when the current is moving quickly. In these conditions, the baitfish become disoriented, especially as the current flow increases and the bigger fish lie in wait to snatch them up. Rips are good places to fish from your boat, but they're also dangerous: The currents can move a small boat around.

REEFS. A reef in salt water not only creates rips but also provides structure for fish to hide in. If you know that a reef runs west to east and the current is moving toward the north, you'll find the feeding fish facing into the current on the north side of the reef. Think like a fish: That's the best place for a big predator to enjoy some protection from the current while also grabbing any smaller baitfish swept over the reef.

THE BIG N

NERVOUS WATER. "Nervous water" is a surface water patch that looks a bit different from the water around it . . .

because something's going on right below the surface. That might mean only that baitfish are swimming around, but it could indicate that bigger fish are chasing the smaller ones around—and that's a good tip for where to throw your lure.

7
MORE GEAR

There is so much spin-fishing tackle available that sometimes it seems next to impossible to know where to start. There are smaller local dealers, major retail tackle dealers with well over an *acre* of gear on display, catalogs with close to 1,000 pages, and Internet sites that can absorb you for hours.

Of course, one of the best ways to decide what bait or lures or other gear you need is to ask a friend who fishes in your area or a tackle dealer who talks to many local anglers. But in the meantime, here is a list of what you're likely to run into as you get started.

WHAT YOU NEED TO GET STARTED	WHAT YOU OUGHT TO HAVE AS WELL	IT'D BE NICE IF YOU YOU HAD THIS, TOO
Spinning reel	Net	Rod case
Spinning rod	Polarized sunglasses	
Line	Wire leaders	
Knife	Fillet knife	
Lures	Rain jacket	
Tackle box	Survival vest or	
Clipper	life jacket (for boats)	
Reel oil	Floats	
and Vaseline	Sinkers	
Hooks	Suntan lotion	
Pliers		
Terminal tackle		

We talked about the most important purchases—rod, reel, and line—in chapter 2. Now here's what you need to know about the rest of the gear.

CLIPPER. A good fingernail clipper, preferably one of the larger, stronger ones that you can use to cut your monofilament line, is a must. It's a lot easier to use the clipper than a knife, and you probably have one at home that you can put in the tackle box. (If at some point you decide to use braided line, you'll need a scissors to cut it. Specialized scissors for just this purpose fit easily into your pocket.)

FLOATS. Plastic floats are usually small red-and-white balls. They come in a lot of sizes and are attached a few feet up your line if you're bait fishing. They keep the bait on your hook suspended in the water, where a wiggling worm, for example, will attract a fish's attention. Keep a couple in your tackle box—one large and one small, depending on how heavy the live bait is. Typically, floats cost a dollar or so.

HOOKS. If you want to bait fish, get a package of hooks. You can get just plain hooks if you want to tie them onto your fishing line; better yet, get hooks with several-inch pretied leaders. These are easy to clip to a snap swivel at the end of your line.

KNIFE. A good jackknife with a couple of blades that can be kept sharp is a necessity and can probably be found at home. You may also want to buy a fillet knife in case you want to clean your catch. A fillet knife has a longer blade than a jackknife; its blade is usually slightly curved as well. Knives vary a lot in price. We advise that you start out with the less expensive models, as they have a tendency to get lost easily!

NET. A small net allows you to land your catch easily and with the least harm to the fish. Expect to pay about $15 for a starter model with an aluminum frame. Nets with wooden frames look better but are generally a lot more expensive.

OIL AND GREASE. Keep a small can of WD-40 in your tackle box to keep your reel running smoothly. Don't worry about lubricating the reel after each use—but it *is* a good idea to spray some WD-40 on the joints after every few uses (be sure to keep the WD-40 off the line). And if you get really ambitious and open the side plates of your reel, pack Vaseline (use this instead of a heavier grease) around the gears. It's best to do this at the end of the season so you'll be ready for next year. WD-40 is available in many stores, as is Vaseline.

PLIERS. Choose needle-nose pliers that ideally won't rust—or, in any case, be prepared to clean your pliers after each trip and spray them with just a little WD-40. Again, there ought to be a set around the house, or certainly at your tackle or hardware store. You'll need the pliers to remove the hook from your catch.

RAIN JACKET. An inexpensive rain jacket will come in handy on a day with showers when the fish are biting well and you don't want to get soaked. Although modern-fabric, high-tech rain jackets are sold for many hundreds of dollars, you can get one for far less. One tip, however: Rain jackets that cost less than $50 are probably a bit *too* inexpensive. They typically don't have all the flaps and snaps necessary to seal you from the rain—and there is nothing much more unpleasant than getting soaking wet and staying that way for a couple of hours.

ROD CASE. If you plan to travel with your gear, get a case to protect your rod. Rod cases made for long air journeys can be expensive, but one that you can just throw in your car will run you perhaps $25 to $50.

SINKERS. If you plan to fish with live bait, you'll probably need sinkers, which you attach to your line to help you cast the bait out a reasonable distance. Sinkers generally come several to a package that costs a dollar or two. A good type to look for has a rubber core within the lead that allows you to attach, remove, and reuse the sinker.

SUNGLASSES. If you buy sunglasses—which can range in price from 20 bucks to hundreds of dollars—get a pair that is polarized. That will eliminate the glare from the water on a sunny day and give you a better view of what's going on beneath the surface. Polarized sunglasses can also increase the contrast in your viewing area, making outlines, particularly those underwater, a lot more distinct.

SUNTAN LOTION. These days, just about everyone should wear suntan lotion. You've probably got a tube at home—don't forget to put it on! The kind that is waterproof and sweatproof is both best and most expensive.

SURVIVAL VEST OR LIFE JACKET. When you're fishing in a boat, have a survival vest (or life jacket) handy. In fact, in salt water the Coast Guard requires kids to have their vests on anytime they're on the water.

TERMINAL TACKLE. You might as well start talking like a fisherperson now. The gear that you tie onto the end of the line is known as "terminal tackle." You don't need a lot of terminal tackle to start; perhaps the most important items are swivels, which will keep your line from twisting. Tie one to your line and you can then attach your lure or bait hook, remove it, and replace it, all without having to tie a knot each time. Just tie the swivel to the line and you're ready to go. Small plastic bags of what are labeled "snap swivels," perhaps 6 to 10 per bag, will cost about $2. The better swivels list the breaking strength right on the bag; look for one that is two to three times the breaking strength of your line.

The only other terminal tackle you might want in the beginning is a wire leader, in case you fish for sharptoothed critters such as pike in fresh water or bluefish in

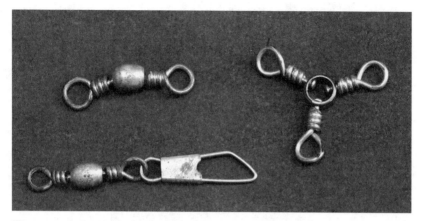

Three varieties of swivels: barrel and three-way on the top, and snap on the bottom.

the salt. The best wire leaders at this stage are about 12 inches long. There's a snap at one end where you clip on the lure or bait hook; at the other is a barrel swivel (two small rings attached to each end of a rotating collar) that allows you to attach your monofilament line to the wire leader. These leaders are typically sold in packages of three to six that might cost $3–4.

TACKLE BOX. A small plastic box is perfect, and these are sold at all tackle stores. You should have a couple of trays with compartments to put your lures, and enough space in the bottom for the rest of your gear. A $10–20 box will get you started.

8

USEFUL WEB SITES

Those of you who surf the Web frequently know that the amount of information there is virtually limitless. When we searched "fishing" at Google, we got 148,000,000 references (that is correct—we mean "millions"!). When we typed in "sport fishing" we narrowed things down to a mere 10,400,000 hits.

So we did a lot of the searching for you to come up with 15 sites that you might find useful if you're new to fishing (kids and adults included). The first two are graded A, because we think you'll learn the most the fastest here—and enjoy the sites as well. The 13 sites labeled B, however, are also quite good and provide plenty of fun reading. Just type the URL into your browser and you'll be off and fishing.

One quick note, however: These sites tend to be modified on a regular basis. You may not find some of the references mentioned here exactly the way we listed them—or you may well find new features that weren't there when we reviewed the site. Still, chances are that the information we mention *is* still around, perhaps under a new heading. Be patient and you'll get there!

FishSA.com (*www.fishsa.com*)   Grade: A

This site is about fishing in South Australia—*but* it's full of well-written tips and explanations that are helpful just about anywhere. It's extremely comprehensive and easy to understand. In particular, on the menu across the top of the home page, check out the sections called "Tackle Talk" and "Reviews"—which you'll find under the heading "Fishing."

"Tackle Talk" contains pieces on all kinds of knots—extremely well illustrated, so that you can easily tie them yourself (this is one of the best knot sections on the Web!). It also has good sections on how to sharpen hooks, how to set your drag, and how to cast. The illustrations are quite clear. The "Reviews" section includes a large number of articles on some very interesting topics such as tides, wind and waves, the age of fish, and so on.

The "Fishing" heading also contains a section called "Boating" that those of you with boats will find worthwhile. In particular, this section is rich with more knot illustrations and safety facts.

One other section to check out on the home page is called "Gone Fishing." Here you'll find recipes, descriptions of many kinds of fish and methods of catching them (fully illustrated), and photos of anglers with their (unusual) catches.

And another thing: Throughout the site are interesting and useful tips to make your fishing more fun and productive. While a lot of this may be more than a beginner can take in, it's good to know that you can find it here when you need it. Some of the information, however, is specific to South Australia.

Fundamentals of Fishing
(*www.angelfire.com/ia3/fishing*)   **Grade: A**
Here you'll find lots of basic information about all aspects of fishing—how to bait your hook, how to clean your fish—all of it excellent for kids, with colorful graphics and engaging, straightforward language. You and your young child can look through this site together and have a lot of fun.

Use the listings you'll find in the column on the left side of the screen to get to what interests you. In particular, "Basic Items of Equipment Needed" is a comprehensive section with many good equipment ideas. "How to Bait Your Hook," also in the left-hand column, makes a sometimes messy process pretty easy. The illustrations in the "Learn to Tie Knots" section are very clear, although a lot of the knots are well beyond what a beginner needs to know. Finally, the section "How to Cast" will further amplify many of the things you have already read in this book and might help make things even easier.

The site has jokes about fishing (pretty silly stuff) and a dictionary of terms that you can use to understand what's what in fishing gear. Again, it's a great Web site for parents to use with their young children as it has a very lighthearted—but not distracting—approach.

ActiveAngler.com
(www.activeangler.com/index.asp)   **Grade: B**

A long list of articles by category on the left-hand side of this home page includes all kinds of interesting information suited for those new to the sport—how-to articles, equipment information, recipes, books, information on conservation, and more.

You'll also find excellent photos to help identify different species of fish, including all common types such as bass, trout, perch, and so on. Descriptions include information on where they can be found, their history, and other facts that make these pieces miniature biology lessons—but very easy to understand!

Fishing Facts
(www.fishingfacts.info/index.html)   **Grade: B**

The list on the left side of the home page—"Fishing Basics"—contains many topic areas where you'll find easy-to-grasp articles. On the right is another set of listings under "Fishing Guides." Also look for descriptions of various types of equipment and fish species (including common baits and lures). The "Fish Dictionary" at the end of "Fishing Basics" has a long list of species that you can click on and study.

The only problem with this site is that the information is quite abbreviated, and it would benefit from more illustrations; still, it's useful.

Utah Outdoors *(http://utahoutdoors.com/ fishing/techniques/index.htm)*   **Grade: B**

While this site was developed for Utah fishing, it's loaded with tips about spin fishing (and fly fishing) that are applicable anywhere. In the middle of the home page is a tab for "Fishing," followed by the heading "Topics." Here you'll find information that's useful no matter where you fish. In particular, check out "Techniques and Equipment," "Fish by Species," and "Techniques." There are many sub-menus with other sites to visit, meaning that there's a great deal of information accessible from this site. There are even fishing stories. The site is written so that anyone new to fishing can enjoy it and learn from it.

GORP (*http://gorp.away.com/gorp/ activity/fishing/fis_guid.htm*)   Grade: B

GORP features lots of basic information, well written and with good photos. At the top of the home page, click on the tab "Activity Guides," then "Where to Fish," and you'll be into all the good stuff.

On the left side of the page you'll find the heading "Fishing Menu"; under that, "Fishing Home," "How To," "Species Info," and "Gear" are all packed with useful information. Numerous articles on all aspects of fishing describe everything from equipment to techniques to places you can go.

GORP is particularly good on the where-to aspects of fishing. There's a map of the United States that you can click on to locate fishing spots near your home. You can even use the site to make travel reservations.

Of all the sites listed here, GORP has been around for the longest time. It's an easy-to-use, mature site.

AskYourCaptain.com
(*www.askyourcaptain.com*)   Grade: B

This has recently become a membership site, but membership is free. Sign in to access this Florida-based site that focuses mainly on Florida and the Bahamas.

On the left side of the home page is a tab called "Main." Under that tab are two categories of contents: "AskYourCaptain Directory" and "AskYourCaptain

Worldwide." Under "Directory," click on either "Articles, Tips and Techniques" or "Seafood Recipes." These pages contain lots of clear and well-written short pieces on many topics of interest to new fishermen. In particular, a section on knots is very well illustrated. There are probably more fishing knots here than you will ever want to know—but at least the drawings are excellent! Although the site concentrates on salt water and advanced anglers, there is plenty of useful information for everyone.

Under the "Worldwide" heading, you'll find subcategories too numerous too mention. In particular, though, look for a listing of fishing magazines and a lot of crucial information on safety.

The Sportfishing Web Site
(*http://mgfx.com/fishing*) **Grade: B**

On the home page, click on "Articles, Internet Resources and Other Information." Here you'll find lots of good pictures to help you identify different species (although the pictures of saltwater fish are far better than those of freshwater fish), tips on releasing fish, and many other articles. One section on shad fishing (particularly on the Delaware River) is very complete if you're interested. It appears that this Web site hasn't been updated for a while—the calendar is loaded with events taking place in 1999. That aside, the rest of the site is okay.

One warning: There is a section called "Really Bad Fishing Jokes." The jokes are truly terrible.

eZine Articles (*http://ezinearticles.com/ ?cat=Recreation-and-Sports:Fishing*)   Grade: B

Here you'll find a whole bunch of interesting articles on fishing for various species and other topics, all written in plain and simple English. How many articles? We have no idea—we stopped counting when we got to 1,000! Indeed, the only problem with the site is its lack of organization. Still, if you're a patient person, it's highly unlikely that you *won't* be able to find a lot of material of interest. A great site for a rainy day!

In addition, when your fishing expertise increases, you can submit articles to this site yourself. You can also sign up to receive articles on fishing as they are added to the site.

Our Media (*www.ourmedia.org/node/76104*)   Grade: B

This is an interesting online video called "Fishing for Beginers 101" with a lot of fishing tips. While designed primarily for saltwater fishing, it's broadly useful as well. There are no articles here, but it's a good way to maintain the attention of kids from 12 to 15. One note: There's a lot of content on the video, and you can't skip to just what you need. You have to watch it all!

FishingMates.com (*www.fishing-mates.com/ fishingbasics/index.html*)   Grade: B

This is another Australian site that also includes a lot of tips applicable anywhere. The site is apparently new, and so there is still more work to be done. Go to the bottom of the page you reach with this URL and you'll see a number of links for more information. If you're interested in knowing how they fish Down Under, this is a good place to visit!

My Fishing Expert (*www.myfishingexpert.com*)   Grade: B

Pretty elementary stuff here, but also some decent tips on all kinds of fishing. This is a pretty extensive site with lots of articles listed on the left side of the home page. Because there are no illustrations, though, this site is probably better for the starting adult than the starting child. You can also search articles alphabetically—not really an efficient way to find what you want, but for those with enough time, it offers a virtually endless source of understandable information.

Bassin' Tips (*www.bassintips.com*)   Grade: B

Here are a great many readable articles on just about every aspect of fishing for bass, one of the most popular gamefish in the United States. The subject listings are on the right and left sides of the home page; there are also two interesting listings in the center called "Anglers Links" and "Fishing Links." These will both lead you to lots of other interesting sites with articles and information about fishing organizations. Unfortunately, there are no illustrations, so you have to wade through a lot of type. Still, it'll probably be worth your while.

World's Best Fishing Tips for Kids (*www.creativeon-line.com/tipsimages/ tipspage2.html*) Grade: B

This is another really good site for young children. The illustrations and language are all very elementary, but the information is quite good. This site will keep a little kid's attention. Many of the drawings, while not heavy on detail, are engaging and easy to follow.

While this site has far less information than any others described here—there are only seven category headings, for instance—that makes it all the easier for kids to follow.

About.com

(http://fishing.about.com/library/

weekly/blnewskidstipshtm.htm)   **Grade: B**

Lots of good tips in easy-to-read format here, though you do have to wade through menus and submenus to find what you want. This site could be better organized to make it more useful. Still, if you're patient, you'll do fine. Look particularly under "Topics" on the left side of the home page.

9

REMOVING A HOOK FROM A FISHERMAN!

Accidents do happen, and you need to know what to do if you get a hook stuck in your partner.

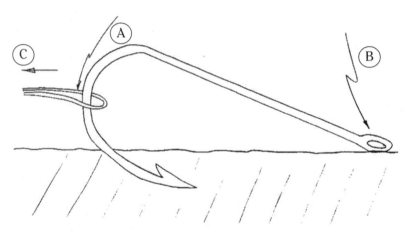

*Quickly, before swelling begins, cut about 3 feet of heavy monofila-
ment line (15-pound breaking strength or stronger) and feed it through
the bend in the hook (A). Grab the two strands of line tightly in one
hand. With one finger of your other hand, press down hard on the eye
of the hook (B). Now tell the "patient" that you're going to count to
three and pull out the hook. Start counting—but on "two," pull hard
on the two strands of line you have grasped (C). (The patient is still
likely to be fairly relaxed at this point, waiting to tense up until just
before you get to number three—which will never occur!) The hook
will come out smoothly, and there should be very little bleeding. Be
sure to wash the site with an antiseptic as soon as possible.*

And one last tip: Wearing sunglasses doesn't just help you see better when there's a bright glare—it can also protect your eyes from a hook heading in the wrong direction!

10

PHOTO TIPS

One of the very best ways to remember a fishing adventure is to take photos. All you really need for this is the kind of camera you can buy in a drugstore for $20 or less. Of course you can also use a super-sophisticated digital camera to put photos on your computer, edit them, and e-mail them to all your friends. (The pics that feature you holding large fish are called "hero shots.")

No matter what type of camera you have, though, always protect it from water by putting it in a waterproof case. For a small camera, that might be simply a ziplock bag.

If you do take fish photos, remember that you have to be fast about it if you intend to release your catch. Hold it in one of two ways: either with a grip in the fish's mouth (be careful of any teeth!) or by putting both hands under it.

Striped bass properly held by the mouth.

Striped bass properly held under the body.

Blue runner.

Bluefish.

Bonito.

False albacore.

Yellowtail snapper.

However you grasp the fish, be sure to use the "Fisherman's Grip"—well out in front of you toward the photographer. That way, it'll look a lot bigger in the final photo!

11

CONSERVATION

One final thought—but it's an important one.

We all have a responsibility to protect our environment. Those of us who spend a lot of time outdoors see firsthand what the benefits of such care are. One way to be sure you're helping our environment is to get involved with groups that work on environmental problems. Many local organizations are readily accessible to you; there are also national organizations worthy of your consideration.

Here's a list of national organizations involved directly or indirectly in fishing and conservation. Take a look at their Web sites for more information and to find out how you can participate and ensure good fishing for many generations to come.

ORGANIZATION	MISSION	WEB SITE
Trout Unlimited	Trout Unlimited's mission is to conserve, protect and restore North America's coldwater fisheries and their watersheds.	www.tu.org
The Nature Conservancy	The Nature Conservancy's mission is to preserve the plants, animals and natural communities that represent the diversity of life on Earth by protecting the lands and waters they need to survive.	www.nature.org
American Rivers	We protect and promote our rivers as valuable assets that are vital to our health, safety and quality of life.	www.americanrivers.org
World Wildlife Fund	WWF's mission is the conservation of nature. Using the best available scientific knowledge and advancing that knowledge where we can, we work to preserve the diversity and abundance of life on Earth and the health of ecological systems.	www.worldwildlife.org
National Wildlife Federation	To inspire Americans to protect wildlife for our children's future.	www.nwf.org

INDEX